Enslow PUBLISHING

BY KATHRYN WALTON

VOL. I From Past to President 1829

ANDREW JACKSON

Please visit our website, www.enslow.com. For a free color catalog of all our high-quality books, call toll free 1-800-398-2504 or fax 1-877-980-4454.

Library of Congress Cataloging-in-Publication Data

Names: Walton, Kathryn, 1993- author.
Title: Andrew Jackson / Kathryn Walton.
Description: Buffalo, NY : Enslow Publishing, [2025] | Series: From past to president | Includes index.
Identifiers: LCCN 2024028828 (print) | LCCN 2024028829 (ebook) | ISBN 9781978542341 (library binding) | ISBN 9781978542334 (paperback) | ISBN 9781978542358 (ebook)
Subjects: LCSH: Jackson, Andrew, 1767-1845–Juvenile literature. | Presidents–United States–Biography–Juvenile literature. | Nashville (Tenn.)–Biography.
Classification: LCC E382 .W235 2025 (print) | LCC E382 (ebook) | DDC 973.5/6092 [B]–dc23/eng/20240702
LC record available at https://lccn.loc.gov/2024028828
LC ebook record available at https://lccn.loc.gov/2024028829

Published in 2025 by
Enslow Publishing
2544 Clinton Street
Buffalo, NY 14224

Copyright © 2025 Enslow Publishing

Portions of this work were originally authored by Michael Rajczak and published as *Before Andrew Jackson Was President*. All new material in this edition is authored by Kathryn Walton.

Designer: Claire Zimmermann
Editor: Natalie Humphrey

Photo credits: Cover (Andrew Jackson portrait) Andrew_Jackson_drawn_on_stone_by_Lafosse,_1856-crop.jpg/Wikimedia Commons; cover (cabin), pp. 7, 15 Morphart Creation/Shutterstock.com; cover (battle illustration), p. 11 Everett Collection/Shutterstock.com; cover (newspaper clipping) STILLFX/Shutterstock.com; cover (Andrew Jackson signature) Letter_of_Andrew_Jackson_to_James_K._Polk.jpg/Wikimedia Commons; cover (author name scrap), series art (caption background) Robyn Mackenzie/Shutterstock.com; series art (green paper background) OLeksiiTooz/Shutterstock.com; cover (newspaper text background at lower left) MaryValery/Shutterstock.com; series art (newspaper text background) TanyaFox/Shutterstock; series art (More to Learn antique tag) Mega Pixel/Shutterstock.com; pp. 5, 7, 15, 17 (ripped blank newspaper piece) STILLFX/Shutterstock.com; p. 5 Andrew_jackson_head.jpg/Wikimedia Commons; pp. 9, 13 courtesy of the Library of Congress; p. 11 Lincoln_Douglas.jpg/Wikimedia Commons; p. 17 courtesy of the Metropolitan Museum of Art; p. 19 JNix/Shutterstock.com.

All rights reserved. No part of this book may be reproduced in any form without permission in writing from the publisher, except by a reviewer.

Some of the images in this book illustrate individuals who are models. The depictions do not imply actual situations or events.

Printed in the United States of America

CPSIA compliance information: Batch #CWENS25: For further information contact Enslow Publishing at 1-800-398-2504.

CONTENTS

President Andrew Jackson. .4
Life in the Waxhaws 6
A 13-Year-Old Soldier 8
The Many Jobs of Andrew Jackson 10
Nashville, Tennessee 12
Rachel Jackson 14
The War of 1812. 16
Finally Becoming President 18
Remembering Jackson 20
President Jackson's Timeline 21
Glossary 22
For More Information 23
Index 24

Words in the glossary appear in **bold** type the first time they are used in the text.

PRESIDENT ANDREW JACKSON

Unlike many other presidents before him, Andrew Jackson didn't start his life wealthy. His **humble** beginnings are one of the reasons Jackson was often called the "people's president."

Andrew Jackson was born on March 15, 1767, in a region called the Waxhaws. Before Jackson was born, his father died and left his mother, Elizabeth, to raise three boys on her own. She decided they would move in with her sister. Elizabeth's sister lived on a farm and had a large family.

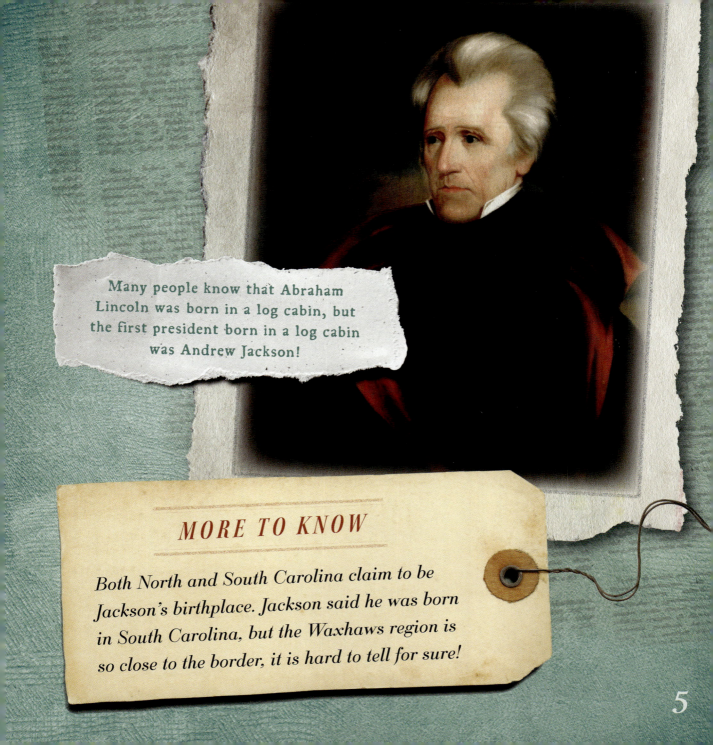

Many people know that Abraham Lincoln was born in a log cabin, but the first president born in a log cabin was Andrew Jackson!

MORE TO KNOW

Both North and South Carolina claim to be Jackson's birthplace. Jackson said he was born in South Carolina, but the Waxhaws region is so close to the border, it is hard to tell for sure!

LIFE IN THE WAXHAWS

When Jackson was old enough to work, he helped on his uncle's farm. Jackson's mother hoped he would work in the church when he was older. But Jackson didn't fit life in the church. From a young age, he became known for playing jokes and fighting.

MORE TO KNOW

Jackson was known to get angry quickly and got in many fights throughout his life.

Although he was a very good reader, Jackson didn't like school. He preferred to skip class and play with his friends. Instead of studying, he'd ride horses and race!

This drawing of a farm worker shows what the young men of Jackon's time may have looked like.

A 13-YEAR-OLD SOLDIER

When 1776 brought the **American Revolution** to the colonies, Jackson's older brothers fought against the British. Jackson later joined the fight even though he was only 13. As a 13-year-old, Jackson and his brother Robert were captured by the British.

MORE TO KNOW

As prisoners, Jackson and his brother Robert both became ill with smallpox. Andrew was sick for many months, but he survived.

THE BRAVE BOY OF THE WAXHAWS.

Andrew Jackson, the Seventh President of the United States, in 1780 when a boy of 13 was taken prisoner by the British. Being ordered by an officer to...

> Jackson had a white scar on his forehead from the British soldier's sword attack. The scar stayed with him for the rest of his life.

While captive, a British officer told Jackson to shine his shoes. When Jackson refused, the officer cut him with a sword. Jackson used his hand to block the soldier's sword. His fingers were cut down to the bone!

THE MANY JOBS OF ANDREW JACKSON

By the end of the American Revolution, both of Jackson's brothers and his mother had died. Now on his own, he needed to find a way to live and work. He tried being a teacher, even though he had not enjoyed school as a child.

At age 17, Jackson wanted to become a **lawyer**. He moved to North Carolina to study with other successful lawyers. He worked hard for three years and eventually earned the right to practice law.

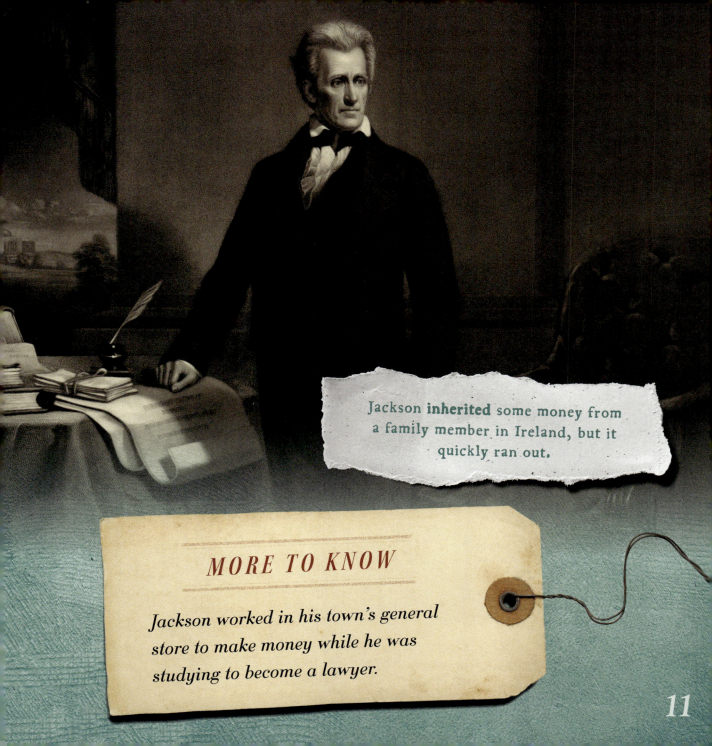

Jackson **inherited** some money from a family member in Ireland, but it quickly ran out.

MORE TO KNOW

Jackson worked in his town's general store to make money while he was studying to become a lawyer.

NASHVILLE, TENNESSEE

In 1788, Andrew Jackson was appointed the **district attorney** of what is today Nashville, Tennessee. His friend and teacher, John McNairy, chose him after McNairy was made a judge in the western part of North Carolina.

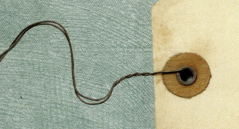

MORE TO KNOW

The area Jackson moved to would become part of the state of Tennesee in 1796.

Jackson traveled through Native American territory on his way west to Nashville, stopping to work as a lawyer along the way. He became known as an honest and hardworking lawyer. He helped many people and often worked to get back money people were owed.

While in Nashville, Jackson bought land and many **enslaved** people to work it.

RACHEL JACKSON

Andrew Jackson lived in a rented room in Nashville. The room was in the family home of Mrs. Donelson. She had a daughter named Rachel. Rachel was married to a man who made her life unhappy. When Rachel left him, she moved back into her family's home. There, she met Jackson.

The two married in 1791. Both thought Rachel's first husband had **divorced** her, but they later found out that he hadn't. After the divorce was completed, Rachel and Jackson were married again in 1794.

Rachel Jackson didn't live to see Jackson become president. She died in 1828.

MORE TO KNOW

Jackson was elected to the U.S. House of **Representatives** in 1796. He became a U.S. Senator in 1797.

THE WAR OF 1812

Jackson became famous across the country during the War of 1812 against Great Britain. Jackson was chosen as the leader of Tennessee's militia. He led troops against Native Americans in Alabama and Florida, winning many battles.

MORE TO KNOW

Jackson was involved in around 100 **duels**. Many of these duels were about his wife, Rachel.

By the end of the War of 1812, Jackson had guarded New Orleans, Louisiana, from the British. Because of his successes, he became a well-known American hero.

Jackson was thought to be strong and unbending as a tree, earning him the nickname "Old Hickory."

FINALLY BECOMING
PRESIDENT

In 1824, Andrew Jackson ran for president against John Quincy Adams. He lost this election, but would run again four years later. This time, Jackson won and became the seventh president of the United States.

In 1830, Jackson signed the Indian Removal Act. This act gave the U.S. government the right to take land that was home to Native Americans for hundreds of years. They were forced to walk for miles to an area across the Mississippi River called "Indian Territory."

Many Native Americans fought back, but were pushed out by U.S. troops.

MORE TO KNOW

So many Native Americans would die on the journey to Indian Territory that it earned the name the Trail of Tears. The U.S. government didn't give the Native Americans food, water, or shelter on this journey.

REMEMBERING JACKSON

Unlike some presidents who came before him, Jackson believed the president should take an active role in government. He introduced **reform** programs to help all white citizens, or people legally living in the country, instead of just wealthy ones.

Before becoming president, Jackson purchased a large piece of land where he built his home. This was called The Hermitage. Today, you can still visit The Hermitage and learn more about Jackson's life!

MORE TO KNOW

Andrew Jackson's ideals about the presidency are called "Jacksonian Democracy." Some of the ideas he believed in are still alive today!

PRESIDENT JACKSON'S TIMELINE

MARCH 15, 1767
Andrew Jackson is born.

1780
Jackson fights in the American Revolution at age 13.

1781
Jackson and his brother Robert are captured by British soldiers.

1781
Elizabeth Jackson, Jackson's mother, dies.

1787
Jackson becomes a lawyer.

1791
Jackson marries Rachel Donelson.

1794
Rachel Donelson and Jackson marry a second time.

1796
Jackson becomes a member of the U.S. House of Representatives.

1797
Jackson becomes a U.S. Senator.

1802
Jackson is made major general of the Tennessee militia.

1804
Jackson buys The Hermitage.

1824
Jackson runs for president and loses to John Quincy Adams.

1828
Jackson is elected the seventh president of the United States.

1830
Jackson signs the Indian Removal Act.

GLOSSARY

American Revolution: The war in which the colonies won their freedom from England.

district attorney: The lawyer whose job it is to start cases against people who may have done crimes in a certain city, county, or state.

divorce: To end a marriage.

duel: A fight between two people that includes weapons and often happens while other people watch.

enslaved: Forced to work without pay and live in poor conditions.

humble: To have a low social position or rank.

inherit: To get by legal right after a person's death.

lawyer: Someone whose job it is to help people with their questions and problems with the law.

reform: Change made to improve or correct an organization, social system, or government.

representative: A member of a lawmaking body who acts for voters.

FOR MORE INFORMATION

BOOKS

Kennedy, Katie. *Presidents Decoded: A Guide to the Leaders Who Shaped Our Nation.* New York, NY: Workman Publishing, 2023.

McKinney, Donna B. *The Presidents Encyclopedia.* Minneapolis, MN: Encyclopedias, 2023.

WEBSITES

Britannica Kids: Andrew Jackson
kids.britannica.com/kids/article/Andrew-Jackson/345484
Learn more about what Andrew Jackson did before and during his presidency.

The Hermitage: Education
www.thehermitage.com/education
Discover more about President Jackson's life and find out how you can visit his family home.

Publisher's note to educators and parents: Our editors have carefully reviewed these websites to ensure that they are suitable for students. Many websites change frequently, however, and we cannot guarantee that a site's future contents will continue to meet our high standards of quality and educational value. Be advised that students should be closely supervised whenever they access the internet.

INDEX

Adams, John Quincy, 18, 21
birthday, 4, 21
birthplace, 6
brothers, 8, 10, 21
church, 6
enslaved people, 13
father, 4
fights, 6
fingers, 9
Hermitage, The, 20, 21
House of Representatives, 15, 21
ideas, 20
Indian Removal Act, 18, 21
marriage, 14, 21
McNairy, John, 12
mother, 4, 6, 10, 21
nickname, 17
North Carolina, 10, 12
prisoner, 8
scar, 9
school, 7, 10
senator, 15
teacher, 10, 12
Trail of Tears, 19